RETAIL MARKETING MANAGEMENT

RETAIL MARKETING MANAGEMENT

Concepts, Guidelines, and Practices

CLÁUDIA BUHAMRA ABREU ROMERO

authorHOUSE®

AuthorHouse™
1663 Liberty Drive
Bloomington, IN 47403
www.authorhouse.com
Phone: 1-800-839-8640

Published by AuthorHouse   04/17/2013

ISBN: 978-1-4817-3944-3 (sc)
ISBN: 978-1-4817-3943-6 (hc)
ISBN: 978-1-4817-3942-9 (e)

Library of Congress Control Number: 2013906626

ENGLISH VERSION OF GESTÃO DE MARKETING NO VAREJO:
CONCEITOS, ORIENTAÇÕES E PRÁTICAS.
Publisher: Editora Atlas COPYRIGHT 2012

Acknowledgments

To my parents, Edson and Sofia,
who always did everything for me!
To my husband, Mauro,
and my daughter, Carolina Sofia,
who are everything to me!

I extend my most sincere thanks to the ones who contributed to
make this book possible:

My family, always present.
And especially, my friends
Robson Gomes and Eduardo Gomes.

CONTENTS

Foreword

The book by Professor Cláudia Buhamra reflects the intense conceptual and practical knowledge of the author, and offers a valuable contribution to retailers of all sizes and industries. This work includes a very complete range of themes for marketing retailers, bringing a wide range of practical examples that are analyzed, updated, and illuminated by solid marketing concepts. Structured in a very didactic way and in a language accessible to different levels of the company, the text facilitates learning and the practical exercise of the themes of retail marketing.

I recommend this excellent book to all retailers who responsibly seek to win the hearts and minds of their consumers.

Prof. Juracy Parente, PhD
Associate Professor in Marketing and Retailing at
FGV-EAESP (Getúlio Vargas Foundation—
School of Business Administration of São Paulo, Brazil)
and the founder of the school's Center for Excellence in Retail.

Preface

I learned marketing at my father's bakery, a business that combines industry and retail. At the bakery, I learned to observe customers and experienced the greatest of all marketing lessons: to understand in order to serve.

When I decided, at age eighteen, to work at the bakery, I had my father's first lesson: you must know well what you sell. I started a course on baking and learned to develop products. I didn't prepare them, but I acquired the skill of creating them and monitoring their execution. The products were carefully designed and tested before being offered for sale. It was necessary to please customers, to stimulate the taste and, above all, to motivate the repurchase. I learned that price is value, because when a product was in fact approved, the consumer was pleased to pay for it.

From an early age, I lived at the bakery the concept of retail attraction radius, because the limit of customer attraction did not exceed five hundred meters without facing competitor that was sometimes stronger than us. I learned to study different and creative possibilities of taking advantage of the flow of traffic, which was not in our favor because the traffic flow was only from neighborhood to downtown. In other words, people passed by car going to work, not home, which certainly hindered the sale of bread. I remember well once when negotiating with an ice cream supplier, we had to change our counter layout because he insisted that the fridge with his brand should be visible to passersby in cars. I learned that day the importance of harmony in *business-to-business* relationships, terminology adopted years later to define the commercial relationship among companies.

At the bakery, distribution logistics were learned as our bakers delivered bread on bikes with speed and skill to ensure that the bread was still warm when received by the end customers or resellers.

The bakery taught me the importance of marketing relationships because the whole neighborhood knew my father and his employees. They, in turn, knew every customer by name, especially those from the book, a primitive and valuable database, now called *database marketing.*

I learned the value of the bakery tastes and the scent of the environment to stimulate the perception of value by customers. At that time, the brand was considered only as a set of letters and figures. People did not think of smells or sounds as components of brands.

Some years after this "school" and graduating from college, I started my academic career and began to teach and write based on what I had experienced and what I believe in: the strength of industry and commerce and the healthy relationship of exchange between buyers and sellers.

The sum of these experiences led me to approach the Chamber of Shopkeepers of Fortaleza (*CDL*) that gave me the opportunity to talk and write about retail marketing in various media.

This book is, therefore, at once the result of experiments, the extent of marketing reflections, and tangibilization of my great pleasure in teaching. And my love for marketing.

The Author

Introduction

To some extent, all organizations do marketing. The issue is that few do it systematically, while others do it sporadically and even intuitively.

Although the title of this book is *Retail Marketing Management*, it aims to provide guidance on business concepts and practices for any business:

- **concepts** that give theoretical support to the ideas expressed herein;
- **guidelines** for the development of marketing practices that make possible the construction of competitive advantages and brand value; and
- **practices** addressed through success stories that serve as benchmarks for other organizations.

Initially we present approaches to define and to show *marketing activities*, including why and how to practice them. Then the *functions of retailers* are addressed and their importance in the distribution of products and services.

The focus then turns to the construction and management of *marks* and excellence in *service* as a way of adding value to branded products and organizations.

Consumer behavior is then discussed, including specifics of the female and children markets.

Aspects relating to *store environment* are also discussed, with emphasis on solving recurring problems in retail, such as *queues' cashiers*, including those in *small retail operations*.

Communication through *sales promotions* and *mobile marketing* are dealt with below, as well as less-commercial, *nonmarketing* communication actions.

For market activities to gain systemization in their planning and execution, a proposed *marketing plan* is presented by which a company *market position* can be defined.

Finally, we present *some useful advice* to readers in the management of their marketing organizations.

Good reading and good business!

Chapter 1
To Start, Recommendations of Kotler

To start, I want to highlight three recommendations given by Professor Philip Kotler in one of his lectures: managing the present, selectively forgetting the past, and creating the future.

1. *Managing the present:* To Kotler, managing the present involves deep knowledge of the environment in which the company is in, including the client and other *stakeholders*, so that managers can make right decisions related to products, processes, and threads, either in the sense of creating them or even abandoning them.
2. *Selectively forgetting the past:* Exploiting accumulated experience is increasingly important in the maintenance of customers and markets. It should include the flexibility to abandon practices that are proven to not represent value for the client nor for the organization.
3. *Creating the future:* For the future, Kotler emphasizes Marketing 3.0, which focuses on the moral and ethical values of organizations, as well as their relation to environmental issues.

The tolerance of new ideas is one of the characteristics that Kotler attributes to enduring companies. For these companies, says Kotler, priorities are: valuing people, not assets; direction and controls that become looser over time; and an organization dedicated to learning and community involvement.

Finally, Professor Kotler summarizes: The ancient philosophy of the relationship between business and society made us believe that "what is good for business is good for society!" The new philosophy, on the other hand, is that "what is good for society is good for organizations."

Thus, we propose to readers to anticipate the future of their organizations from the ideas presented here and practice planning marketing that enables the effective management of the present and the selective forgetfulness of what has passed.

Chapter 2

After All, What Is Marketing?

Initially we are going to understand the etymology of the word *marketing*, and then explore it as an administrative activity.

> MARKET   ING
> MERCADO   LOGY

The word *mercado* comes from the Latin language and means "market." The English suffix *logy* comes from the Greek language and means "the study of." So, mercadology means "the study of the market."

However, studying the market is just the beginning of the process, because the marketing activities in a company originate *after* the market is researched. By possession of knowledge about the characteristics of target customers—their needs, desires, and purchase behaviors—the company can be prepared to serve them.

The American Marketing Association (AMA) defines *marketing* as "the activity, set of institutions, and processes for creating, communicating, delivering, and exchanging offerings that have value for customers, clients, partners, and society at large" (AMA 2008).

It is possible to summarize the definition of marketing and its activity as follows:

> Marketing is the organization response to the demands of consumer, through adjustments performed in their operational processes.

In the first part of the definition that was presented—*marketing is the organization response to the demands of the consumer*—an adaptation of the definition given by Jerome McCarthy and William D. Perreault Jr. (1960), one of the precursors in marketing studies, two words deserve to be highlighted: *response* and *demand*, because they point to the actions of marketing directed outside of the organization. Considering that you can only answer correctly when you know the question, it is impossible to promote the satisfaction of the client without knowing his needs and desires. This means researching the market and getting closer to the reality of the customer to have a greater chance of success in offering products and services that satisfy him.

In the second part of the definition—*through adjustments performed in their operational processes*—we stress the words *adjustments* and *processes*, which point into the organization. That is, after knowing the market, we must prepare ourselves to serve it. And that includes the company as a whole, not just the marketing area. From the president to the janitor, everyone should be oriented for the customer.

In short, marketing is the activity that builds brands of value in the market by offering products and services with a focus on the expectations of its effective and potential customers and on organizational objectives.

Chapter 3
And What Is Not Marketing?

After defining marketing, it is worth clarifying what marketing is *not*. We call this conceptual clarification.

First, *marketing is* not *a fad*, because no fashion would last so long and would not develop with such strength as occurred with the subject of marketing within the context of science in business administration.

Marketing is not *just propaganda*, as some still think it is. In fact, advertising is the marketing tool that most appears, that most stands out, because it happens in front of the cameras. Nobody sees what happens when the company is planning or conducting market research. People do not take note of the anguish experienced by executives and businessmen in developing new products. People do not take note of what they live as they decide the price of a product or its distribution to become competitive and accessible to the consumer.

But everyone sees the advertisement. It is on the billboards, in magazines, in newspapers, on packaging, and on television, among other media that surround us daily.

Marketing is not *fooling people*, under any circumstances. That's lack of ethics and respect, shame, not marketing. Some even make false advertising, but this is a distortion of the concept of marketing. Marketing has, in essence, the honest-exchange relation from company to consumer, based on win-win, not win-lose, as some assume.

Marketing does not *finish with the sale*. The sale process is just the beginning of a relationship that should last for a long time, if it is in the interest of both sides. The moment of the sale is the confirmation of the promise made by the company in the media. The satisfaction is just confirmed later, and repurchase depends on this satisfaction.

What gives longevity to companies in the market is the continuing relationship they have with their customers. As the relationship progresses, the client represents less cost to the organization, because it is not necessary to invest in order to win him and there is less risk of default when you know the reputation of the one with whom you negotiate.

Marketing is not *just for big companies.* Moreover, the smaller the company, the greater is the chance it will have to be closer to its customer, to hear him, to exchange ideas and learn about him. Of course, when you give examples of marketing actions, large organizations' brands are known by more people, but that does not mean that only large corporations are able to do marketing.

Marketing is not *just for private companies.* There are many public companies that do good marketing, all over the world, through logistics efficiency, product development, and targeted custom or environmental actions that contribute to the construction of brands' market value.

Marketing activities have been equally important to the Brazilian government to stimulate the correct and healthy behavior of the Brazilian population, such as the practice of prenatal testing, prevention of prostate cancer and breast cancer, and respect to traffic safety, including the use of helmets, seat belts, and child safety seats in the backseat, as well as campaigns against alcohol for those who will drive.

Finally, it is worth mentioning that *marketing is* not *just for companies that seek profit.* NGOs—nongovernmental organizations—as well as some charities demonstrate commitment to the provision of real value to society.

Having made these conceptual clarifications, we can move on to analyze the activities of a marketing professional.

Chapter 4
What Are the Activities of the Marketing Area?

Many theories are supported by paradigms that are meant to facilitate their understanding and operationalization. So it is with the *mix* or composite marketing or simply the 4Ps (product, price, place, and promotion), which represent the pillars of marketing activity. But what is the origin of the *marketing mix*?

The concept of *marketing mix* was designed in the fifties (Grönroos 1994) by Professor Neil Borden of Harvard Business School.[1] In 1964, he authored an article entitled "The Concept of the Marketing Mix," which was published as a chapter in the George Schwartz's book entitled *Science in Marketing* (Borden 1984).

The marketing mix created by Borden (1984) originally contained twelve elements. They are:

- **Product**—quality and design appropriate to the target market;
- **Pricing**—price policy;
- **Branding**—brand policy;
- **Channels of distribution**—channels between producers and consumers, and efforts to ensure harmony in the channel;

---

[1] According to Prof. Borden (1984), the term mix was inspired by Professor Culliton James, who, in 1948, in a study of marketing costs, described the executive as a "mixer of ingredients" that sometimes follows recipes created by others, sometimes creates his own recipe, sometimes adapts recipes to ingredients already available, and sometimes experiences or invents new ingredients never tested before.

- **Personal selling**—sales staff;
- **Advertising**—how much to spend and the platform to be adopted of product and company image;
- **Promotion**—special plans for sale;
- **Packaging**—decisions about packaging and labels;
- **Display**—methods of exposure of products and communication pieces that help the sales process;
- **Servicing**—decisions on necessary services;
- **Physical handling**—logistics (warehousing, transportation, and inventory);
- **Fact-finding and analysis**—acquisition, analysis, and use of data in marketing operations.

In 1960, Professor Jerome McCarthy and William D. Perreault Jr., in their book *Basic Marketing: A Managerial Approach*, presented the twelve elements of the marketing mix proposed by Neil Borden synthesized in four variables beginning with the letter "P," making the "mix" known as the 4Ps of marketing: *product*, *price*, *place*, and *promotion*.[2]

In the concept of the product were included attributes of the product itself, branding, packaging, and servicing, as listed by Borden. The *price*, which involves, in addition to the amount paid by the customer, payment methods and deadlines, among others, is equal to Borden's term of pricing. The *place*, whose best translation is distribution, includes the decisions of channels and logistics

---

[2] Although McCarthy has popularized the concept of the marketing mix as four Ps, in 1956, Harry Hansen divided the marketing mix into six elements (Grönroos 1994): product policy, channels of distribution, advertising, personal selling, pricing, and selling program.

distribution of products, services, and information to the client that Borden called physical handling (storage, transportation, and inventory). And, in the element *promotion*, or communication, are the variables of advertising, sales promotion, personal selling, and display, also listed by Borden. Finally, fact-finding and analysis, cited by Borden but not directly included in the four Ps, gives supports to all marketing operations with acquisition, analysis, and use of market information.

These four elements of marketing—product, price, place, and promotion—on the one hand facilitated the understanding of the subject, but on the other, they brought a problem of definition of the functions of the marketing professional. After all, we cannot imagine a person or department responsible for all of these elements, whose management involves different areas and functions within an organization.

What occurs in most organizational structures is that decisions on the product are made in the areas of R&D (Research and Development) and production. Issues relating to price are under the responsibility of finance. Distribution is handled by the area of distribution and logistics. Finally, communication is the responsibility of the marketing area, as shown below.

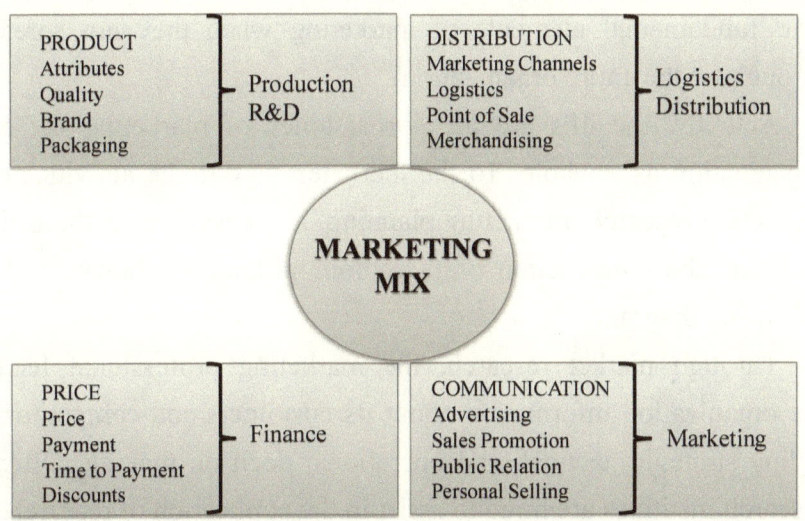

However, professionals in the media, including advertisers, make advertising, sales promotion, and public relations assignments. Personal selling, in turn, is another form of marketing communication, which most often is handled by an area known as sales management or business management, as shown in the diagram below.

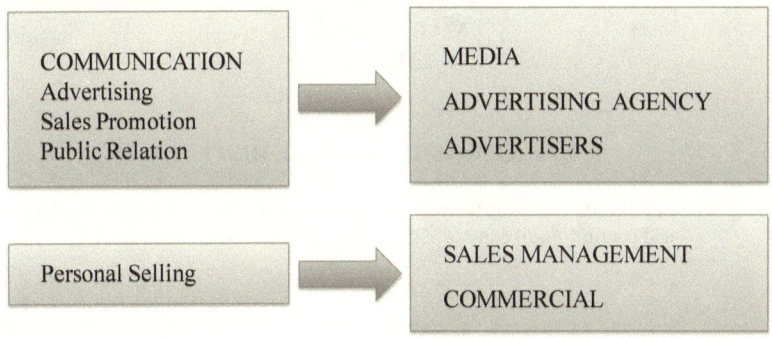

Given this reality, what are the functions of the marketing professional? How is it possible for this professional to work the four fundamental elements of marketing when they are spread throughout the entire organization?

Actually, the 4Ps are the cornerstones of marketing for an organization as a whole. To the marketers is due the activities of marketing research, marketing planning, and customer relationship to guide the construction of these four pillars, as shown in the following diagram.

Through market research, the marketing professional feeds the organization information about its customers and competitors, aiding strategic, tactical, and operational decision making. Often, research institutes are hired to assist in the application of research.

MARKETING RESEARCH = Brings information about the marketing: competitor and customers (preferences, rejections, beliefs, attitudes and behaviors).	**MARKETING PLANNING** = Helps all areas of the company to define actions that deal with the needs, desires and clients expectations in a competitive way, and monitor its results.

FUNCTIONS OF THE MARKETING AREA

RELATIONSHIP MANAGEMENT = Being in constant communication with the clients to measure and promote his satisfaction and controlling all contact points of the company with its market.

With the planning activity, the marketer directs all actions relating to product, price, distribution, and communication developed by the various organizational areas, integrating them into the concept of customer focus. Mason, Mayer, and

Wilkinson (1993) added, though, two Ps they called compound retailer: *Presentation*, or point of sale (also included in P: Place or distribution), and *People* (considered in all marketing pillars). At the moment of marketing planning, it can be helpful to have consultants who can contribute to the construction and implementation of the plan without employment that sometimes compromises the mechanisms of execution and plan control.

Finally, with the relationship activity, the marketing professional brings to the company the "voice of the customer" and takes to him the organization's response.

Even when there is not formally a marketing area in the company, its activities must be present, seeking the ultimate goal of building value brands, winning and keeping customers, and ensuring profitability for the organization.

From Borden's and McCarthy's messages, we conclude that the 4 Ps—*product, price, place,* and *promotion*—together form the pillars of the marketing of an organization, but the responsibility of its construction involves all who are part of it.

Chapter 5
Why Do Marketing?

One of the most frequent questions in the corporate and academic environment concerns the real need for a company to do marketing; after all, marketing actions for achieving and maintaining customers not only require time for planning, but also financial resources for their implementation. It would be easier if organizations devoted their time and resources just to selling and making a profit without much effort being devoted to it. But things do not work this way.

It has become increasingly difficult for successful market relations to happen spontaneously. There is a lot of effort necessary for achieving and maintaining clients, who have become increasingly demanding.

Now let's talk about some of the many reasons why organizations should do marketing. We will discuss, first, changes in consumer behavior, then changes in competition, and finally, the actions of the state.

5.1 Changes in Consumer Behavior

There is no denying that the consumer has changed. Oversupply beyond demand in the market has put numerous options in front of the consumer. Sales are appealing from all sides. The packaging, promotion, advertisements, new products, everything are reasons to seduce and delight consumers.

But the fact is that they are not so easily seduced, and delighting consumers has been one of the most arduous tasks of marketing management.

What is this new consumer like? Below are some of the characteristics of the consumer of today:

More demanding
More selective
More rational
More unfaithful
More well informed
Enjoys personalized treatment
No time available

Customers are more demanding; there is no denying that. They ask for and charge everything. They want the best offer, with maximum convenience at the lowest price.

Customers are more selective. They select products, brands, stores, salespeople, prices, and payment methods. All that is offered to the consumer goes through a rigorous selective process of options so there is no regret in relation to the purchase made.

Customers are more rational. Rationality is expressed, for example, by opting for the most expensive product because it ensures greater reliability at the time of a repair, a service need, a complaint, or even a repurchase.

Customers are less faithful. Today it has become common to use the term *customer loyalty*. But, in essence, what does the word *loyalty* mean?

According to the dictionary, loyalty is to be faithful, to not change, to not use something else. It means that if a consumer is in fact loyal to one brand of a product, he will not use another brand of the same product category. Likewise, if you are loyal to a store, such as a supermarket, you will not buy anywhere else but there. It's the extreme, but this is the real definition of the word *loyalty*.

Making a client loyal is, therefore, one of the most difficult activities of a company, particularly because the consumer of today loves novelty and, in most cases, cannot resist the many temptations to try the new. There are many offers. And by the time he experiences such offers, he has already left the idea of being faithful. Some might say it was just to prove a point. Nevertheless, the concept of fidelity was damaged.

It's the same thing that happens in marriage. Can a husband or wife call himself or herself faithful, but "try new things"? Even if it is "only once"? The same thought applies to the trade in which the concept of loyalty is involved.

Others might argue that the client tries something new, but returns to the old provider, the old product, the old shop, the old seller. Then we face another concept: the preference. This one is better suited for today. If a company can gain consumer preference, it will have many advantages over the competition. Moreover, *to prefer* means continuing with the supplier despite knowing others. Preference may even generate loyalty. But it is loyalty that must be won first.

The customer is better informed. There are many media that lead consumers to understand their rights and the defense mechanisms at their disposal. The Internet brings the ability to compare products from many different suppliers from different places in the world without leaving home. It is free, accessible information.

Customers currently enjoy personalized treatment. Nobody likes to be treated without individuality. Faith Popcorn, in her book *The Popcorn Report*, published in 1992, already pointed out, among other things, the trend of *Egonomics* as the consumer brand of the twenty-first century. It is the idea that "no one is like me."

Finally, we can state that the *consumer of today has no time. Incidentally, time is the most expensive resource today*. We can no longer make the consumer waste time on a phone line that does not access the credit card, or parking lots always crowded or with unprepared vendors. Every day consumers migrate their "boring," daily purchases to the Internet. Purchases made in person should have an effect increasingly playful, pleasurable, funny. Consumers want to live a new and delightful experience every time they go shopping. And that will be the big challenge for companies in the future, especially for retail ones.

5.2 Changes in Competition

In addition to the observed changes in the behavior of the customer, compelling reasons to do marketing have also been submitted by the competition, which:

Hard

Diversified

Strong brands

Quality as obligation

Searching for the differential

Competition is fiercer and more diverse. Competitors are not always those that make or sell exactly the same product as you. A competitor is any product or service that disputes the financial resources of its potential customers. Or, as Walt Disney said, "A competitor is any company with which your customer compares you." Winning the competition requires creativity, innovation, and above all, an incredible desire to serve. This reality makes marketing essential for organizations of any kind, public or private, in an environment of competition or monopoly.

Another relevant aspect in the evaluation of competition as a reason for marketing is increasing investments in *creating value brands*, which are what really win customers. These are the brands that give meaning to trade, now increasingly focused on emotion. The greatest asset of your organization is your brand, whose value is determined by the respect and admiration it inspires in its customers. The less it pleases its audience, the less value your company brand has in the market.

Besides the brand, there has been much talk about competing on quality, but *quality today has turned into obligation*. We must *seek differentials* to be noticed. Offer a good product, serve well, and provide good service are the minimum conditions to exist as a company. Otherwise, one is vulnerable to the wrath of the consumer market that today is more demanding and better informed and enforces its rights through legislation that protects and media that investigate companies.

5.3 Actions of the State

It isn't only customers and competitors that justify the marketing investment of the organization. The actions of the state are also significant, sometimes inspecting, sometimes punishing, sometimes educating. The state has these three types of power:

> Supervisory Power
>
> Punitive Power
>
> Educational Power

The state oversees organizational actions that may undermine the free negotiation between buyers and sellers. It also punishes when it identifies bad faith in actions that cause harm to the consumer.

Through specific laws, such as the Consumer Protection Code, the state also directs paths to lawful activities of organizations in the market.

By marketing, the company develops focus on the customer and respects his needs and emotions, thus becoming, less vulnerable to anger and formal complaints of the consumer. By marketing, the organization adds focus *on* the customer to the focus *of the* customer and seeks profit by satisfying its external and internal customers. By marketing, the organization constantly reviews itself from the perspective of the customer and continuously reinvents the pleasure of serving.

Marketing, however, cannot be a sporadic activity within the organization. It requires systematic planning of several actions, among them the preparation of people to work with competence and pleasure.

Chapter 6
How to Do Marketing?

Now that we understand *what* marketing is and *why* to do marketing, let's see *how* to do marketing.

6.1 Treating the Customer Differently

The first lesson of how to do marketing is:

> Identify the differences of each client.

The expression "every customer is equal" refers to a pattern of common behavior of all types of consumers, such as a requirement for proper care, respect for their rights, and respect for the veracity of the purposes of the company.

However, it is essential to identify the differences among clients or among customer groups. The process of grouping customers with similar characteristics is called market segmentation. The next step is to identify the individual characteristics within the segment. After all, even with similar social and cultural characteristics, individual differences, defined by personality, values, and the story of each person or entity, are what define the unique style of being and behaving.

Once we understand the behavior of the segment and its participants individually, it is important to keep in mind that the market cannot be judged, but needs to be understood and met.

6.2 Giving More Reasons Than Price for the Customer to Buy

The second lesson of how to do marketing is:

> Understand that the customer
> does not purchase price only

We cannot deny the importance of price in the purchase decision process. The price is a measure of fair exchange between the resources of the consumer and the supply organization. But what is fair in the buying process? It's fair when the buyer gets more than a product, when the brand is symbolic communication that conveys confidence, problem solving, satisfaction, and delight.

There are numerous market-leading products that are not the cheapest. *Havaianas* sandals, a Brazilian product, are a good example. For many years, when they were cheap, they were devalued, sometimes exposed in empty cardboard boxes thrown in a corner of grocery stores. When they redefined their colors—and initially only the colors, because the raw material of the flip-flop sandals today remains the same—*Alpargatas* repositioned the brand in the market, redefining the distribution channel, communication, and price, which got higher. And they sold more. Much more. Then came new designs and success increased, as well as price and sales. And now they are sold internationally. They are a global product.

Definitely the customer doesn't purchase by price only. The great challenge of the marketer is to make the price a measure of fair exchange and deliver value consistent with the price charged for the product.

6.3 Don't See as a Competitor Only the Ones Who Make the Same Product

The third lesson of how to do marketing is:

> Realize that competitor is not just the one
> who does the same as you do.

Currently, one of the greatest difficulties of organizations is identifying who their competitors are. They can arise from more distant places and through various activities.

Shopping on the Internet has redefined the market configuration. No one talks about *marketplace* anymore, but *marketspace*. There aren't anymore geographic areas that define the competition, but rather the availability of substitute products sold through physical contact or virtually.

The Coca-Cola Company, for example, doesn't see as a competitor only the soft drink makers. Because of this, it has expanded its portfolio of products into water, juice, sports drinks, and tea, among others.

Walt Disney extended the concept of *competitor* when he said that "A competitor is any company with which your customer compares you." This means that competition can be in the product, in the central office, or in the performance of service and punctuality of an organization.

6.4 Disseminating the Concept of Marketing Throughout the Organization

The fourth lesson of how to do marketing is:

> Disseminate the concept of marketing throughout organization because every business is a chain that has the strength of the weakest link.

The people who make the organization at all levels must understand and internalize the concept of the brand and the importance of serving the customer, since they are fundamental in generating value to the market. And it's from the direction of the company that the example should start.

6.5 Knowing the Customer and Evolving with Him

The fifth lesson in how to do marketing is:

> Innovate and evolve with the customer.

The greatest demonstration of modernization of companies is through the knowledge of the changes in their market and the adjustment of supply of products and services to these changes.

Tracking and even anticipating market development allows the company to go beyond the focus *on* the customer to the focus *of* the customer, discovering in each evolutionary process what the customer hopes for from the organization's performance.

6.6 Defining Metrics to Measure the Effectiveness of Marketing Actions

The sixth lesson in how to do marketing is:

> Establish the expected return of each
> marketing investment.

No longer are investments permitted to be made without outcome measures, especially in the area of marketing. The less quantitative results previously used by professionals, such as level of brand *recall*, remain important, but are no longer sufficient if they're not set in return sales, revenue, and profitability.

6.7 Be 100 Percent Ethical

The seventh lesson in how to do marketing is:

> Build the brand based on ethics.

The greatest asset of an organization is its brand, which is more than a symbol. The brand is a compound of meanings that expresses the company's conduct toward its employees, suppliers, customers, competitors, and all its *stakeholders*. Being 100 percent ethical, besides being a requirement, is the safest way to ensure the longevity and success of the organization.

The following chapters present diverse marketing actions that can be implemented as a way of making marketing work in your organization.

Chapter 7
The Importance of the Retail Function

The importance of retail is undeniable. It would be very difficult if all products were distributed to final consumers by the manufacturers themselves. They would have an unthinkable logistics problem, and the customers themselves would live right next to the doors of their homes due to the constant visits of suppliers. Although all manufacturers might choose to have their own retail stores, the cost would rise a lot, which would reflect negatively on the prices of final products.

In this scenario arises, then, the figure of the retailer, who buys to resell, who assumes the risks of storage, thus providing invaluable service to society. Notice in the following figures two possibilities for product distribution, one with and the other without the presence of the retailer.

DIRECT DISTRIBUTION

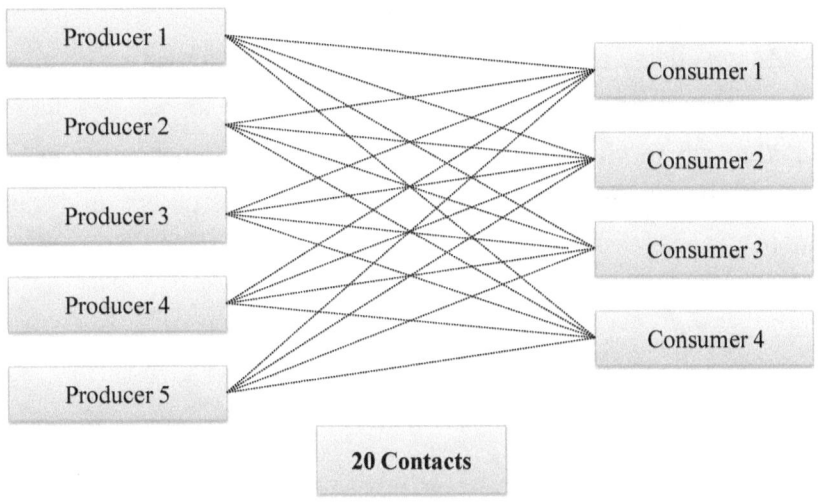

DIRECT DISTRIBUTION

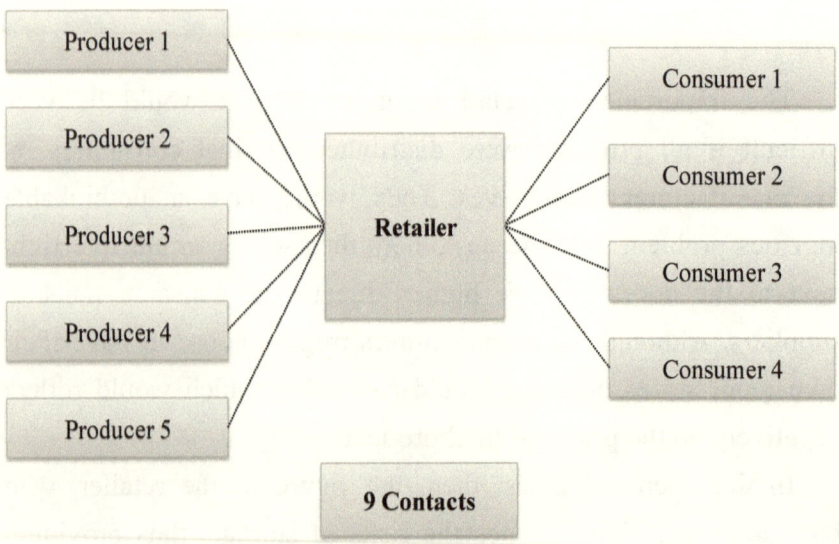

But why, then, in the face of such great importance, do retailers sometimes face many difficulties in trying to survive? The answer to this question can be found in one word: *service*. What is missing for most retailers is seeing themselves as manufacturers of services, which is much more than just providing products.

As resellers, retailers do not differ from each other. But as service providers, the possibilities of customer loyalty are huge. It is through services that the differential of retail competitiveness lies. These are the services that delight, win customers, and gain loyalty.

Source: www.shutterstock.com

Recently I was looking for a washing machine. I undertook a pilgrimage among appliance stores in the city; and in them all, I found the same service: technical, cold, focused on the capacity and price of the machines. I noticed the same automation in all vendors, who were more concerned to give me a card in case I decided to buy it later, than in solving my "problem."

To start with, no one asked me where I would put the machine. Yeah, that seems like an obvious question, but it's not, because I wanted the machine at my beach house, which should direct my search to machines with a higher composition of plastic, because of the salt air of the place. But this was a "detail" that I had to discover by myself, investigating the various types of machines on the market.

Many retail professionals—and here we include enterprises and employees—miss the perception of the business from the point of view of the customer. Satisfied customers will give you preference in future purchases and also give your name to other buyers.

The more you identify the need that prompted the customer to visit the store, the faster and easier it gets to adequately supply the customer's needs and hence close the sale, the ultimate goal of negotiation.

Chapter 8
The Creation of Strong Brands in Retail

Professor Theodore Levitt (1985) said that people do not buy products, but solutions to their problems; and this fact, for many years, guided the industry in product development. Allied to a great brand, products present a growing number of differences in performance that make buyers and users loyal.

Source: www.shutterstock.com

But in retail, how can you make customers loyal? The answer to that question is: through *branding*, the building of retailers' brands with value in the market. Building brands generates a combination of names and symbols that make sense to the consumer as a symbol of respect, awe, and confidence. Through strong brands, companies take a privileged position in the process of the consumer's purchase decision. They enter into what we call the "consideration set," formed by the brands that are in the forefront of buyers' minds at the moment of choice.

In retail, brands are built through the *mix* of products and offered services, their prices, their outlets, their employees, and their suppliers, all of which must be in perfect harmony with the intended audience. Through brands, companies form attitudes and positive behaviors in people about their supply in the market.

Attitudes represent a predisposition of a person in relation to something or somebody and shape the person's behavior. There are three dimensions of attitude: the cognitive, the affective, and the conative dimensions (Karsaclian 2004; Solomon 2002; Engel, Blackwell, & Miniard 2008).

The *cognitive dimension* refers to the knowledge that the individual has on product brands and organizations. At this level of attitude formation, companies must create opportunities to present their purposes, their products, their prices, and finally, their value proposals as market *players*.

The *affective dimension* refers to feelings that consumers feel in response to certain brands. The emotional aspect assumes an important presence in purchase decisions. Liking or disliking a particular retailer of a product will shape the intention of purchase, conation, the third dimension of attitude.

The *conative dimension* represents the intention of the potential consumer to act in relation to a particular product, service, or organization.

Thus, the attitude formed in the levels of cognition, affectivity, and intention will determine the individual's way of acting. In other words, purchase behavior derives from the knowledge, feeling, and intention that consumers develop regarding product brands and organizations.

The steps of the Hierarchy Model Learning Standard (Solomon 2002)—know, like, buy—occur in reverse sometimes in sales promotions in which individuals buy what they don't know and, sometimes, even what they don't like. These sales promotions generate sales and they can be useful in specific situations, but only the construction of strong brands leads the customer to loyalty and, hence, leads to the financial sustainability of an organization over time.

Chapter 9
The Stakeholders of the Brand

Building and positioning brands valued in the market is one of the biggest goals of marketing activity.

The brand, a combination of name and symbol, represents the identity of a product or an organization. It is also one of the most important techniques of market communication due to the range of meanings expressed in terms of quality, performance, durability, reliability, price, and user status, among others.

As a corporate identity, the brand communicates to the target audience the company's intended positioning. Through forms and colors, smells and sounds, the brand now occupies a prominent place in the minds of those who compose the market, defines competitive differentials, and makes promises that create expectations in buyers and other *stakeholders*. And to meet the expectations of *stakeholders*—employees, suppliers, customers, society, owners, shareholders, and managers—should be the mission of all organizations. This is common sense.

However, if serving the *stakeholders* is the enterprise's mission, it is necessary—and equally important—to engage them in the process of construction of the brand. A mission is up to each *stakeholder*, as follows:

Source: www.shutterstock.com

Employees: Internalization of the concept of brand, by the employees or outsourced employees, is indispensable for the definition and adoption of an ideal model of dynamic performance. It is in contact with the posture and verbal and visual speech of employees that the brand is perceived and accessible by customers. This absorption of the brand concept by employees of an organization usually doesn't occur spontaneously. It requires investment in training and internal communication to share organizational goals.

Suppliers: Suppliers are also responsible for the companies' brands that they sell; companies are their organizational customers. *Recalls* of defective products by suppliers are not rare. The big problem of these *recalls* is the impact on the brand image of the product and its producer, rather than the suppliers, which often cannot be identified due to their lack of proximity with the final market consumer.

Customers: The joint construction of the brand with clients has gained much strength from interaction *sites*. The newest way of idea generation, called *crowdsourcing*, uses the intelligence and collective and voluntary knowledge spread on the Internet to create products and solutions and even develop brands.

Society: As a *stakeholder*, society expects from companies more than an efficient product or the satisfaction of their needs. In an organized manner, society now is concerned about human dignity and the environment, so they look to the guidelines of Marketing 3.0. While Marketing 1.0 was focused on product and Marketing 2.0 on consumer satisfaction, Marketing 3.0 expands its focus to the welfare of society in the long run, interacting with it in building value deals.

Finally, *owners, shareholders,* and *managers* must understand that building a brand involves *all* stakeholders, and engage themselves in fulfilling the mission, vision, and values of the organization.

Chapter 10
The Scent of Brands

Including scent in a brand is a practice already used by some retailers.

Formed by the combination of words and symbols, brands identify products and organizations, representing safety in the purchase and repurchase stimulus (Ferrell & Hartline 2009).

Historically, the components of a brand are name, the part that can be verbalized, and symbol, which cannot be verbalized. Later, sounds were added to brands through *jingles*. And more recently, scents have become an important part of brands.

The scents, beyond promoting remembrance and identification of the business, as do the other components of the brand, have the purpose of expanding the customer experience at the time of purchase. A pleasant smell can inspire wellness and relaxation, contributing to more pleasurable choices.

A survey held with 146 people about olfactory marketing—the practice of inserting scent into brands—showed that 25 percent of the people interviewed linked the scent presented to the respective brand. Among actual customers, the percentage of remembrance increased to 85 percent (Torres & Buhamra 2011). Most importantly, they remembered the scent and the brand with a feeling of satisfaction and pleasure.

Source: www.shutterstock.com

Working the scent into spaces has become so significant that it even interferes in the logistics of some retailers. In supermarkets, for example, bakeries were always placed at the end of the store to cause the daily flow of customers through the shelves of other products until get the bakery. Currently, some supermarkets are placing the bakery at the front of the store since they understand the contribution of the irresistible "smell of bread" to attracting customers.

In this context, even employees should be careful with the aroma they exude, whether in clothing or in the perfume they wear. They should beware of bad breath and the odor of perspiration. Everything matters, because "retail is detail."

Chapter 11
Differentiation Through Services

The challenge for industries to differentiate themselves in the market has become increasingly bigger. And for many reasons. One of them is oversupply. Every day consumers are exposed to numerous different proposals of diverse suppliers that promise the better price, the better product, the better way of payment, and the better treatment, among other advantages.

Source: www.shutterstock.com

The fact is that as offerings increase, the level of demand and expectations of the customer also increase. What once charmed them becomes the basics. What used to be called quality has become an obligation. The basic benefit of a product is the minimum that must be offered in the market. Refrigerators must conserve food well. Pens should write well, and they can't burst inside bags, as used to happen in the past.

Today we live in a process called commoditization. That is, all things have become *commodities*, similar products, with little perceived differentiation. Manufacturers need to make an effort so their products can offer some real differential to the market and that is sustainable over time.

The retailer, in turn, suffers the reflections of this reality, because if products and brands sold in store A are the same as are sold in store B, what will make the buyer decide between store A and store B? Price is one of the choice factors, but the option of the customer is not always the cheapest price. Quality care and additional services, or supplementary services, as Lovelock and Wirtz have demonstrated (2006), weigh in today's purchase decisions much more than low price. It is through service that the stores should make the difference, going up to the customer, saving his time, and offering convenience, facilities, and enchantment.

In addition to products, customers buy the confidence and security that there will be a friendly attitude after sales if the products have defects and it is necessary to exchange them. The security of having a partner, more than a product, is today the decisive factor in the choices of the consumer.

But service requires a lot of planning and perfect execution. How do you plan service? The initial step is to know your target audience and know what is really important for him. Creating services from creative *insight* can be valid, but very useless if the customer doesn't consider them important.

The next step is formatting a quality service and determining where it will run: in the store or in the customer's home. There must also be close attention to costs, because not every additional service may be free and customers will be willing to pay for it only if they perceive it is valuable.

Finally, an important decision is who or what will be involved in providing the service, whether people or equipment. When it comes to technology, it is good that it works, especially if it is self-catering.

As for people, proper training is essential. It is necessary to educate everyone involved in the execution of service how important their service activity is for customer satisfaction, for the development of business, and for their own professional development.

The sum of all these efforts aims, ultimately, to generate *good value*, which, as explained by Juracy Parente (2000), will mean it will be "worth it" for the consumer to buy from you.

Chapter 12

Postures in Customer Service

Dealing with the public, either in person or by phone, is something inspiring. But it is necessary to like to serve, to solve problems, and to learn in order to upgrade oneself. The proper posture is also necessary. In serving an external customer or an internal client (employees, work colleagues), some rules are important:

Education: Being educated means being polite and gentle. This is not a favor, but an obligation, not only as a professional, but also as a human being. And everyone knows it. What happens, though, is that sometimes, involved in the processes of everyday life, people forget to smile or to use softness in their voices. What cannot be forgotten is that, although it is already the tenth customer of the day, for example, to that tenth client it is the first time. One must understand that each client is unique and each situation is unique, just as you are professionally. No one can be nice for you. No one can build your image in your place. It just depends on you.

Clothing and slang: Another aspect that everyone should worry about is the way they dress and express themselves. Whether you wear a uniform or not, care with clothing reflects care of oneself and respect for others. Our clothes work as packaging, through which is revealed the quality of our content as professionals and as official representatives of the company.

Source: www.shutterstock.com

After all, the employees are an extension of the brand for the company where they work. And just as care with appearance is important, language is part of the appearance. The use of slang or vulgar expressions is as indelicate as the use of technical terms that only you understand. Before giving any information, ask if the client knows what it means. And then make sure that he understood. You'll save time and will be much more effective in reaching results.

Know how to listen: If being able to speak is important, being able to listen is even more important, because knowing how to listen prepares one to speak. Without knowing the client's needs, it is difficult to satisfy him. Always satisfying the customer does not necessarily mean doing everything he wants. On the contrary. Listening prepares you to say no, but in a gentle way. Put yourself in the customer's place. Stand beside him, involved in the process to solve his problem. And listen calmly and with attention. Many times, an angry customer is unarmed when he finds someone to hear him. In fact, his anger is not against you, because he does not even know you; it is against the unknown, against his impotence to solve a problem that, sometimes, is so simple.

In service, gentleness and a smile are ingredients that never fail. They are good for external clients, for internal customers, and above all, for those who want to provide good service.

Chapter 13
How to Sell Well in High Season

Retail activity is seasonal. Vulnerable to annual events, retail sales may fluctuate up or down, leaving purchasing professionals a challenge to predict, with the greatest possible accuracy, the levels of sales of each season.

In seasons with recessions, promotional actions are very welcome, both for those who buy and for the ones who sell. In these moments, companies try to earn the consumer preference of those who are not motivated and have few financial resources to purchase.

As for the seasons when the motivations of consumption are spontaneous and sales are high without much effort to convince consumers—like Mother's Day, Father's Day, Children's Day, and especially Christmas—attention should be given not only to the quantity that is sold, but to the way contacts between buyers and sellers are made. After all, we cannot see festive occasions only as opportunities to increase sales, but as times to win new customers.

These moments, unlike what it seems, require as much attention from the retailers as recessive moments.

Considering the large number of people who will be circulating in the store, some caution is recommended to promote fast and efficient service:

Source: www.shutterstock.com

1. A suitable quantity of attendants, especially store cashiers, because very long lines may cause withdrawal from buying and resistance to more purchases.

2. Personal empowerment, not only as regards professional aspects, but also emotional control and personal behavior, because the intense movement of purchases during special events can generate wear on employees, who should be valued and motivated in order to not show feelings of tiredness or moodiness.

3. A varied *mix* of products so that customers can have shopping options.

4. Organization of the store so that the logistics of treatment can be suitable to evaluation and choice of the products.

5. A nice ambiance, including decoration, lighting, and a sound system, which do not interfere in the process of the

buying decision, but create a feeling that it is nice to be in the store.

These recommendations do not apply only to gift stores, such as toys, clothes, shoes, accessories, books, jewelry, watches, and housewares. They also apply to supermarkets and construction material stores, pharmacies and pet shops. They also apply to providers of services, such as hairdressers, laundries, hotels, bars, restaurants, and amusement parks.

Do not turn the pleasure of shopping into torture, but into pleasant experiences that bring a positive impact to the business throughout the year.

Chapter 14
Exchanging Products for Customers

I believe that there is no longer anyone who doubts the importance of the exchange of products to win and keep customers. Although not all kinds of exchange are specified in the Consumer Protection Code, this practice is already ingrained in the culture of commerce. Exchanges are done by kindness when no defect in the product or its origin is noticed.

What is striking is that even in such an obvious area, there are still companies that do not know how to deal with this practice, and what is worse, create rules that keep clients away more than attract them.

Recently I was faced with three situations that illustrate different ways of approaching the problem of exchange:

Case 1: I went to a store for children to exchange a piece of clothing and was surprised with the information that it would not be possible because the date of exchange had already expired. As I had not realized that date was on the label, I had to accept the argument of the seller, although I was a bit indignant. It was true, after all, that the piece of clothing had been bought a little over a month earlier, but it still had the label. But I had no argument or excuse. I resigned myself to the store's decision.

Case 2: I bought a swimsuit for my daughter, but my daughter, although only nine years old, knew exactly what she did not like and she did not approve it. I had to go back to the store to exchange the swimsuit. As I had difficulty choosing another swimsuit, the store manager suggested I come back the next weekend, when they would have already received a new collection and I would have more options of exchange. I was delighted. At the end of the week, I returned to the store, as agreed, but I was surprised with the information that the swimsuit was worth 20 percent less because of the arrival of the new collection. It was now on sale. I was lucky, though, in that the manager remembered me and agreed to contact the company to be allowed to give me the full credit, which could only be done on Monday. I waited and returned to the store, and the exchange was conducted.

Source: www.shutterstock.com

Case 3: On another occasion, also to exchange some clothes for children, I was served by a friendly salesperson who greeted me with a smile that did not disappear from her face upon learning of my goal. Although the exchange date had expired, she explained that the date was important to keep track of collections, but even with a few days of expiration, there was no reason to deny my exchange request. I loved it! And I bought more! And I was charmed with it all. It was a true experience of marketing, which now I share with you.

These are examples that show how flexibility and empathy can change relationships and bring solutions. Case 1 caused me so much embarrassment that I will never feel the desire to return to that store. In case 2, although the solution did not happen in the first moment of the attempted exchange, the demonstration of interest by the manager for my case comforted me. When I returned, 20 percent no longer represented much loss because she showed she "was by my side." However, she went ahead and got authorization to reimburse me the full value of the exchange. Finally, case 3 illustrates perfect service. It's important to recognize that it is not always possible to demonstrate that level of flexibility, but empathy is essential in any situation.

It is necessary to empower the front line to deal effectively with clients who come for an exchange as well as the one who comes to buy. After all, one thing leads to another. Exchanging products for customers is one of the easiest and most inexpensive marketing strategies to win customers and make them loyal.

Chapter 15
Your Majesty, the Consumer

We live in the age of the consumer. And this is not new anymore. We created new forms of care, enchantment, and customer relationships, seeking to generate differential competitiveness for our organizations. The expression of the day is "value perception." We need to create value to be preferred by our customers and be able to keep them.

The big challenge, however, is to understand what is value for customers, and more, to understand how this concept of value changes over time. What was appreciated one day is not anymore, and won't be tomorrow, especially when all competitors now offer the same benefits and what was different and unique is now common for customers, who now demand more from their suppliers.

Today's consumer loves novelty. Serving and charming him requires continuous interaction with him. It is necessary not only to research him formally, but to informally approach him and record everything that is said for a more adequate future offering to meet his needs and desires.

That requires a lot from the staff, especially the front line, where sellers are the eyes and ears of organizations. It is necessary to know how to listen and speak in full measure to access not only the customer's pocket, but also his mind and heart.

Source: www.shutterstock.com

Today's consumer sees the act of buying not just as a utilitarian relationship, but as an experience to bring him pleasure, raising self-esteem and satisfying some of his needs. He wants, constantly, to try the new, which requires from companies an enormous capacity to reinvent themselves to appeal to this consumer, who shows, every day, new expectations regarding products and services.

In the nineties, the American consultant Faith Popcorn introduced, in her book titled *O The Popcorn Report*, trends that would shape the twenty-first-century consumer. These trends are a reality now:

Cocooning: The desire to be alone at home, making it a comfortable and safe cocoon, which brings companies the challenge of going up to their customer, bringing him convenience and time savings.

Fantasy Adventure: An escape from daily tensions, through trips, food, and programs on virtual reality.

Small Indulgences: The search for multiple ways to reward oneself by relieving stress, satisfying little quirks that express "I deserve," giving space to the creativity of organizations in serving them.

Egonomics: A kind of pleasant narcissism, through which people seek some recognition that "nobody is like me," emphasizing the personalization of products and services.

Cashing Out: Work in excess leading men and women to appreciation of the simplicity of things and life in the pursuit of happiness.

Down-Aging: Nostalgia for childhood freedom, leading to certain types of consumption behaviors that are more relaxed and products that once were great successes.

Staying Alive: Increasing awareness of the concept of well-being that helps to reinforce the ideal of a better quality of life, including the adoption of foods and healthy habits.

The Vigilant Consumer: Increasing consumer awareness, leading to greater pressures on unethical actions of organizations.

99 Lives: The accelerated pace of people, forcing them to fulfill various roles and admit that they may face a very busy life, dominated by technology, giving space to multifunctional devices such as cell phones that shoot pictures or gas stations and pharmacies with large diversification of products and services.

S.O.S. (Save Our Society): A social conscience whose core elements are ethics, passion, and compassion for the environment and society as a whole.

In line with the predictions of Popcorn, more recently Beth Furtado, a Brazilian advertiser, launched a book titled *Desejos Contemporâneos (Contemporary Wishes)* (2008), which portrays the paradoxical behavior of the current consumer, who wants to stay home but has desires of socialization, as well as worries about the environment, but does not give up the convenience of disposable things.

On the one hand, this new consumer wants what he does not have, but only for a short time, making ephemeral the sense of novelty when obsolescence happens in the time of purchase. On the other hand, this new consumer emits signs of fatigue and asks for less—less product, to reduce the stress of doubt; smaller stores to decrease the time spent on the purchase; and simpler processes to make life lighter.

There are therefore, great challenges for companies that want to serve and delight this consumer who, regardless of age, each day presents new behaviors. But there are also certainly great opportunities for those that can anticipate, disseminating knowledge and the importance of the customer throughout the organization.

Chapter 16

The Female Market

The empowerment of women was one of the great changes of the past fifty years. Today women make up the majority of professional workers in many countries, 51 percent in the United States, for example (The Economist 2009).

According to the United Nations (2010), the share of women in the labor force gives an indication of the extent of women's access to the labor market relative to men's, and a value of 50 percent indicates gender parity. Most regions of the world are still far from attaining this, but there has been progress, most notably in Latin America and the Caribbean. In South America, women now comprise 44 percent of the labor force, compared to only 33 percent in 1990.

Brazilians number 190,732,694, of whom 51 percent are women (IBGE 2010). Brazilian women already represent 45 percent of the workforce; 35 percent are heads of families. They have more years of education (8.3 years versus 7.5 for men), and live longer, with a life expectancy of 76.3 years, while for men it is 68.3 years.

These data, which reveal the growing importance of women in the national scene, force us to give special attention to their role as decision makers and influencers of purchases, as well as consumers, although, on average, they still have lower salaries than men.

Selling for women has become increasingly necessary and challenging. Regardless of income level or social class, women have become increasingly more demanding. They demand rights and question obligations.

Understanding and attending women implies being tolerant with their inquiring, researcher mind. Women do not buy in the first store. They have, by nature, a process of purchase decision that takes longer than that of men. Whether deciding on a restaurant menu or buying clothes, building materials, or textbooks for children, they need time "for a spin" until they decide what or where to buy.

Source: www.shutterstock.com

Women often demand differentiated services, such as a space for children that allow them more freedom for choices. Or for companions, with the same goal.

Women love going to the shopping mall or to the street trade, without commitment, just to "unwind." They appreciate shop windows and environment aromas. They integrate with sellers, exchange ideas, and ask opinions.

But one fact, however, is indisputable: women have less and less available time for shopping, imposing upon organizations the challenge of adding quality of service to speed, courtesy to objectivity, sympathy to assertiveness, and lightness to determination. The excellence of marketing to women today is through the combination of features seemingly contradictory, but effective. As is the female soul.

Chapter 17
The Challenge of the Children's Market

How to sell to children? Unlike what you think, selling products for children is as or more difficult than many categories of products intended for adult audiences. First, because the child is increasingly an early decision maker regarding purchases; from the age of three, children are able to choose products, especially in bakeries and supermarkets.

The other difficulty arises from the number of people involved in this decision-making process, which, obviously, does not happen individually. That is where the purchase roles appear—the initiator, the influencer, the decision maker, the buyer, and the user, as identified below (Kotler & Keller 2006):

Source: www.shutterstock.com

- *Initiator:* The one who first gets the idea to purchase a product or service;
- *Influencer:* The one who influences the purchase decision;
- *Decision maker:* The one who decides the product and brand to be acquired;
- *Buyer:* The one who actually pays for the product purchased; and
- *User:* The one who actually will use or consume the product purchased.

As you might expect, until the age of three years, the only role taken by the child is the user. From that age, however, parents start to ask some questions, offering opinions and suggestions, entering the child into the universe of influencers. In this stage, children also assume, in some circumstances, the role of initiator when requesting the purchase of a product, such as toys, cookies, candies, and chocolates, for example. And then comes the moment when the decision is entirely in their hands, in the purchase either of food or technology. And the role of decision maker becomes increasingly frequent as the child, over time, develops his or her personality.

Given this reality, some issues stand out to producers and sellers who are active in the child universe. First, it is necessary to create space to experiment, to live the experience of shopping in the store, both for parents and children. After all, many purchases today can be done without leaving home. Secondly, opportunities should be created to make the child want to go back to the store, through specific offerings supported by a complete and updated database. Finally, vendors must deal with the child universe as an act of love, understanding the language that best convinces and delights them.

Chapter 18

"No, Thanks. I'm Just Taking a Look."

It has been a great challenge to reconcile sales goals with relationship actions. Are our sellers prepared? How should they act when the clients say they are "just looking"?

Perhaps the solution to this dilemma is in the form of compensation from the front line. With excessive focus on sales, organizations tend to use only quantitative and financial metrics to measure the performance of their sales force, which, before a good offer to the market, should not need so much force to sell.

In order to adopt a new approach that values all customers, including those who are *just looking*, two major changes are required by the company.

The first one is starting to see the client beyond his financial value. For this, the management must initially establish the mission of the organization and disseminate it so that everyone can share the same desired future for the company. This must go beyond remuneration to capital; it must be the result of a job well done, not an end in itself.

New performance indicators should be established alongside the sales goals, such as: number of new won customers, number of new registered customers, number of customers contacted in the period. These are actions that generate good business and they go beyond immediate sale.

Source: www.shutterstock.com

The second change to be made to value the customer who is only *taking a look* is to invest in training salespeople to focus on the study of consumer behavior, so that by understanding it, companies can better serve customers and even sell them more.

As for sellers, it is important that they engage in understanding how people think and shop, as a final consumer or representing a company. One of the most interesting chapters of consumer behavior concerns the steps of the buying process (Engel, Blackwell, & Miniard 2008).

Initially the client passes through the *awakening of need*, a process that can be started inside or outside the store. Then comes the *search for information*. Right now, the preparation and patience of the seller make the difference. Anxiety for selling only disturbs the customer. The customer does not need to intend that he will buy. He is gathering information and should get details up to his expectations.

The third stage is the *evaluation of alternatives*. It is at this moment that the good attendants are being considered for closure of business. Those who just want to sell, who are not engaged to listen, and who suffocate or despise the client certainly will be excluded from this process of evaluation of the alternatives of purchase.

Finally come the moments of *purchase, consumption, and post-purchase*. The purchase occurs after the customer decides to exchange his financial resources for the company's offer; the consumption, when he uses the product purchased; and the post-purchase evaluation summarizes the feeling aroused by the whole experience lived during the process of purchase and consumption. Satisfied, the customer will come back. And he chooses the store. And he becomes loyal. Remember, he is exactly the one who was "just taking a look."

Chapter 19

The Power of Small Retailers Focusing on Consumer Behavior

Strategic alliances between large retailers have been common. The question for small retailers is: How do I compete with giant groups with enormous buying power and the ability to sell at low prices?

The answer can be found in two important approaches in the study of consumer behavior: *value perception* and *market segmentation*.

The study of value perception reveals that price is not the only element that decides the purchase. Price is important, but it alone does not decide about the purchase of a product. It is possible that in a given situation, the client sees more benefit in paying little when the product is not very significant, but he is willing to pay more for a quality service that gives him security in case he needs the company on a post-sale basis.

All that matters in a negotiation is how the customer perceives value of the organization's offering in exchange for his money. You can raise the perceived value of products through staff, technology, processes, and your company's brand. When the perceived benefit is bigger than the cost of purchase, the customer not only pays more, but also tends to be loyal.

Source: www.shutterstock.com

The technique of market segmentation, in turn, drives the company's market division into smaller groups of consumers with similar characteristics. Then the company chooses to attend to one or more of these consumer groups, also called market segments. Formerly, the market was sliced, or segmented, based only on demographic variables—such as gender, age, and income—or geographic variables, such as neighborhoods, cities, states, regions, and countries. Today, market segmentation also takes into account benefits and behavioral moments. That is, the same customer, at a certain moment, may see advantage in a big store with several options of products, not caring about the time that will be required for his process of purchase decision—and in another moment, pressed by the scarcity of time and patience, he may opt for smaller shops, and even higher prices, favoring speed and convenience.

As Professor Francisco Madia, from ESPM—Escola Superior de Propaganda e Marketing (Higher School of Advertising and Marketing) says in his lectures, every consumer has his generic and his specific side. At a given moment, the client wants to be just another person, anonymous. This is his generic side, highlighted in major department stores. In another moment, however, he wants to be recognized as someone special. This is his specific side, which is identified with minor shops with more specialized care. And it is exactly the specific side of the consumer that small retailers can focus on with differentiated and customized treatment and services.

What the customer searches for is the meaning of the purchase, risk reduction, increasing his safety, and above all, personal identification with the vendor who offers him adequate care that meets his expectations at the time of the purchase.

Chapter 20
Beware of Lines!

In just one week, I twice witnessed people giving up their shopping in lines at the cashier. And great buys! The first occurred in a women's fashion store in a mall in São Paulo, and the other, in a supermarket in Fortaleza. In both situations, the people left raving, complaining, and instigating other people in line to leave. And I was one of them!

I was listening and reflecting on possible reasons that lead some retailers to not give due attention to the line of the cashier. After all, the purchase process is only effective after the payment for the products. And until that point is a long way to be covered: we must look for products, choose what to buy, sometimes trying them on and going up to an attendant to ask questions. And in the end, in both of these situations, because of a long line at the cashier, the purchase process ended in frustration. The customer's boredom led him not to take what he chose, what he wanted to buy.

Actually, no matter how great the products, how inviting the prices, how prepared the sellers, and how spectacular a shop environment, if, at the time of closing the sale transaction, the customer stays interminable minutes, which seem like hours, in queues to the cashier, he will get upset and wonder about the real usefulness of the purchase: Is it worth spending that money at that time? Would it not be better to skip it? Or spend it on a better offer? Or in a better shop?

Source: www.shutterstock.com

Recently, a survey with fifty-one customers at the exit of a large department store (Celestino 2012) showed that forty-nine of them dropped out of the purchase process because of the line. And all were with the products they wanted to buy in their hands or in the cart.

Some of the customers didn't even get in line, a phenomenon known as *balking*. The others entered, but withdrew from the purchase after some time in the line, a phenomenon known as *reneging* (Haight 1957).

Annoyed, the customer goes, then, to buy in a competitor store, with a sweet taste of revenge, an attitude that weighs negatively on the company's brand and imposes on the entrepreneur a great challenge: besides measuring his sales, he should measure what he stopped selling.

The flow of customers in retail shows daily seasonality, which must be addressed in an effort to avoid unwanted congestion in the store environment. Some steps are recommended regarding both the organization and the number of checkout lines, such as qualifying people who perform this function, which includes not only sympathy, but also technical skill.

There are famous queues like the ones at the parks of Disney, which have already transformed themselves into experiences for customers while they wait. Or the ones from some restaurants like the famous Famiglia Mancini in São Paulo, providing the chance for customers to enjoy the delights of food and beverage menus while waiting for a table.

In banks and some government agencies, there are already available chairs and televisions to minimize waiting in the lines.

At some retailers, such as clothing, toys, supermarkets, bookstores, and pharmacies, just to name a few, giving up a purchase may not represent much to a customer, but over a period of time, this will generate significant losses of good opportunities for the business.

Chapter 21
The Atmosphere of the Store as a Marketing Tool

In 1973, Professor Philip Kotler, a well-known author in the area of marketing, wrote an article entitled "Atmospherics as a Marketing Tool," which underlined the importance of the atmosphere of the store to the welfare of customers and, therefore, business success.

Source: www.shutterstock.com

Professor Kotler said that a pair of shoes, a refrigerator, a haircut, or a meal are just a small part of what the consumer buys. What he buys is called the total product, which comprises the services, guarantees, packaging, advertisements, payment methods, kindness, images, and other factors that accompany the product. One of the most significant elements of the total product is the location in which it is bought or consumed. In some cases, the atmosphere in the place influences the decision to purchase more than the product itself.

Although his text was written forty years ago, this is a topic about which there is still some ignorance on the part of some entrepreneurs, who do not understand the importance of the store atmosphere as a marketing tool for the enhancement of selling.

At that time, the author pointed to two reasons for this neglect. The first is that some entrepreneurs are very practical and functional in their thinking, which leads them to not appreciate the aesthetic questions of a purchase. Another factor is that the atmosphere of the environment comprises the silent language of organizational communication, often not considered before the verbal language.

According to the dictionary, the atmosphere is the layer of air surrounding the earth. In marketing, it refers to the air that surrounds the store. A pleasant atmosphere reinforces the possibility of purchasing, in the same way that an unpleasant atmosphere, confusing or depressing, may discourage the purchase.

But what makes up the atmosphere of the store? The sensory dimensions of the consumer are the components of the atmosphere, as detailed below:

- In the visual dimension are the colors and all the merchandising techniques: internal and external signage, decoration of shops and storefronts, logistics in the provision of exhibitors and products, and so on.
- In the hearing dimension, there are the sounds from environmental music, equipment, internal acoustics, or the neighborhood.

- In the olfactory dimension, there are the scents, whether from the brand itself or from external elements like the perfume of sellers or customers, or food consumed in the store.
- In the tactile dimension, there are the touches, the textures, and the environment temperature.

The dimension of taste, though not directly interfering in the atmosphere since this cannot be tasted, can be enhanced by serving beverages and light foods as an additional courtesy to the consumer.

Once the composition of the environment is decided, it is necessary to assess whether the atmosphere as perceived by customers matches that desired by the company, for it must be appreciated and understood in its essence by the customers in order to trigger the wanted emotions and generate the expected results.

Chapter 22
How to Communicate with Your Market

It is the desire of every entrepreneur, especially retail entrepreneurs, to see his company in the media. And this is indeed a legitimate desire, so as to attract the attention of a consumer and remind him of the company at the time of purchase.

The promotion, one of the elements of marketing (see chapter 4), covers four forms of communication: advertising, sales promotion, public relations, and personal selling (Kotler 2006). Consider the characteristics of each one of these forms:

Advertising: Advertising is any paid form of nonpersonal presentation and promotion of ideas, products, or services, performed by an identified sponsor. The objectives of advertising are: to inform, persuade, and remind. The advertisements can be institutional, when publishing the company's brand; product, when the goal is to introduce one or more products of the company; or promotional, when used for the dissemination of any sales promotion at any given time.

Sales promotion: Sales promotion consists of short-term incentives designed to stimulate immediate purchase of a product or service, and can have as objectives to induce the experimentation with new products, increase sales in a period of low demand, or gain exposure within a preferred point of sale, among others. More details on sales promotions are in chapter 23.

Public relations: This function is connected with the direction through which a company seeks to obtain and maintain an understanding and friendliness of all those with whom it has or may have a relationship. Public relations are the spokesperson of the company. In large organizations, the role of PR is very important in the activities of press relations, with suppliers, with some customers, and even with politicians. In medium and small companies, PR activities may be carried out by the owners, if well prepared for this role.

Source: www.shutterstock.com

Personal selling: Personal selling is the interpersonal element of promotion. It consists of a two-way communication between sellers and customers, whether in person or by other means, such as telephone, videoconference, or the Internet. To be good promoters of the company, salespeople need, above all: to know the company and identify with it; know the company's products; know the characteristics of the customers; know the characteristics of competitors (but never speak bad things about them); and know how to make an effective sales presentation.

As important as the way of communication is the decision about the media to be used. Whether for sale to the final consumer (business to consumer) or to the organizational buyer (business to business), penetration of the media in the market intended is what will determine, in part, the success of the communication.

The right choice of media, whether mass (television, newspaper, radio, outdoor), selective (websites, paid TV channels, specialized magazines, press office), or customized (direct mail, e-mail marketing, telemarketing, mobile marketing), presupposes a good knowledge about the target audience that will be exposed to your message.

For this reason, it is vital that you deliver your company's communication from a professional on communication. Although people in your company or in your family draw very well and are very creative, do not assign them the responsibility of creating pieces for the communication of your brand, unless they are knowledgeable in the art of advertising communication. Also, leave the responsibility for developing your media plan to a professional in the area, although you may have a good feeling about what is required.

Finally, before investing in communication with the market, one of the four elements of the *marketing mix*, the entrepreneur should pay close attention to the other three Ps: product, price, and point of sale. Communicating before "cleaning the house" means you will reach more people to see your mistakes.

Chapter 23
Sales Promotion as a Marketing Tool

Sales promotion is a tool of marketing communication that aims to stimulate sales immediately. One of the characteristics of the promotion is the time limitation, that is, to be believed the promotion must have a determined time to finish; otherwise, it will not generate the immediate demand that is expected.

Source: www.shutterstock.com

Promotions are usually sporadic and utilized only in specific situations, such as periods of low demand or changes in the collection such as the liquidation of inventories. There are, however, daily promotions which everyday a different product is put on sale. Discounts are very common, as well as free samples, coupons, raffles, an extra amount of products and offerings, or "take three, pay two." Sponsorships—sports, social, cultural—are also classified as promotion.

A new version of "promotion lightning," as these quick promotions are called, are collective purchases via the Internet, through which companies offer discounts up to 90 percent on their products and services that are purchased by groups of people from different locations, but with common interests.

But if on the one hand, these promotions have the advantage of directly stimulating the buying behavior of consumers, on the other hand, this same advantage can represent a threat if the demand response stimulated is not managed properly, which can generate frustration for consumers and damage the reputation of the organization.

It is common to hear stories of discrimination from customers of collective shopping sites in restaurants and other service companies. As the purchase of products and services over the Internet represents a vote of confidence by consumers who believed in their virtual offer, buyers who become disappointed at the moment of getting what they bought and feeling cheated, promise never again to buy from the same vendor, and even denigrate the image of the organization. It is necessary to train the front line well to achieve customer loyalty in times of promotion, not only the occasional sale.

With daily or sporadic promotions, some cautions should be observed when adopting sales promotions:

1. Offer a real advantage for the customer. He knows how to evaluate if the promotion is beneficial, and this encourages him to purchase.

2. Beware of the material used in gifts that bear the name of your company. After all, your brand is the most precious thing and should not be linked to poor quality gifts.

3. Know your audience very well to suit the promotional offer to their characteristics. Selling for children, for example, may require an appeal to more recreational activities, such as popping balloons to win prizes.

4. Show the products in promotion in an attractive way. Crowding them in front of the store can embarrass the customer in choosing what to buy and reduce the effect of promotional activity.

5. Disclose the developed promotion in an attractive way. The promotional advertisements are just as important as the offers, after all, is useless promote and not advertise.

6. Finally, beware of the structure of your company, so you can efficiently meet the demand generated by your promotion. If you announce discount prices, you should take care that the logistics service for the increased demand does not harm the quality of service; frustrating the customer can mean losing him forever.

It has already been proven that promotion increases sales, but it takes process management so that its effectiveness can be measured not only by increased sales, but also by success in winning new customers.

Chapter 24
Mobile Marketing: Advantages and Care in Its Use

While the mailer accesses the consumer via correspondence, printed or electronic, and telemarketing accesses him via the telephone, fixed or mobile, mobile communication joins the two forms and sends text messages via cell phone. This is mobile marketing, the newest form of direct marketing.

The growing use of mobile phones is promising for mobile marketing, or portable marketing. ABI Research indicates that the global market for mobile marketing will jump from $1.8 billion in 2007 to $24 billion in 2013 (HSM Online 2008).

There is no doubt that accessing a consumer via message SMS—Short Message Service, at the moment he is strolling through the mall, inviting him to come into your store, can be very effective, mainly for sales promotions. But this kind of message has been more useful for institutional messages. Actions post-sales can also be valuably delivered via SMS, a powerful instrument of relationship marketing (Weyne & Buhamra 2009).

Communicating by phone has many advantages, among which are: low cost, customization and privacy of messages, and how quickly they arrive to the recipient. However, research shows that consumers have resistance to this form of communication, and only 14 percent like to receive advertising by phone (Malozzi 2010).

Source: www.shutterstock.com

Therefore, so that mobile communication functions effectively, some precautions are necessary. First, the messages should be short to facilitate reading and understanding their content. Second, it is essential to maintain an updated database so that messages do not migrate to the wrong cell phones. A third caution is the definition of some form of performance measurement of communication, because without measuring results, any action, even if it is cheap, will represent waste.

And finally, so that the action is received amicably by the consumer, when you are completing the registration of the customer, you should ask permission for his cell phone number to be used for sending messages from your business. This type of market action is also known as permission marketing, and without permission, any message sent will be characterized as an invasion of privacy, which may reflect negatively on the image of the organization.

Chapter 25
Nonmarketing: Actions Beyond the Market

The concept of nonmarketing is growing. According to David Bach and David B. Allen (2010), professors of IE Business School in Spain, nonmarketing covers deliberate strategies beyond the market, designed to create business opportunities in the social and political environment. In other words, it is about actions developed in politics, environmental policy, or social policy, that, at first glance, have no direct relationship with the company's business, but contribute to building a respected brand admired by its current and potential customers.

Source: www.shutterstock.com

According to Bach and Allen (2010), investments in nonmarketing strategies are driven by four factors:

1. *Multiple audiences:* Historically it was argued that a company should adapt to the laws and customs of the countries where it operates. However, with globalization and virtual social networks, even if a company operates only in one city, the repercussions of its actions have effects beyond the physical boundaries, which forces all entrepreneurs to observe concepts of universal ethics for the preservation of their brand and business.

2. The *globalization of nongovernmental organizations:* Not only have companies become global, but so have ideas, people, and NGOs as well. With the power of images, emotions, and media, NGOs are always vigilant at reporting spendthrift practices, regardless of company size.

3. *New regulatory hurdles:* As opportunities have arisen across borders where companies operate, threats have also emerged from laws that govern trade relations in different market environments, about which organizations should be aware.

4. *Competitive edge:* In all sectors, increased competitiveness is visible, either equal products or substitute ones. Actions beyond the market can make the difference in winning and keeping customers.

The concept of nonmarketing is related to all efforts of the company that do not generate immediate profit and do not appear to be directly linked to the buyer's market. However, they are strategic actions directed to build a solid brand. They are environmental protection actions or of social benefit that show to the market the "soul" of the organization, for which profit is a result of a good job and not an end in itself.

History has shown that companies with socially responsible souls have a chance to survive the growing level of demand from stakeholders, being customers, shareholders, suppliers, or employees themselves.

Caring for the environment or social environment allows the company to achieve simultaneously multiple market segments, audiences of various ages, income levels, or social groups, without distinction. After all, this is a topic that benefits everyone, including those who are not interested in it.

Political and operating practices that enhance the competitiveness of a company while improving the socioeconomic conditions in the communities in which the company operates are what Porter and Kramer (2011) call "shared value." They say: "You must reconnect company success to social progress."

However, so that work really functions, it is indeed necessary that actions are real and the results of legitimate concerns. It is not good to adopt schools, communities, or areas of environmental preservation, for example, only to "appear beautifully in the photo." Consumers know the value of true actions and repudiate the false ones.

The benefits of environmental investments also extend to internal customers. Being part of a company that has other goals besides profit arouses positive feelings of pride in employees and partners.

Chapter 26
A Practical and Effective Model of a Marketing Plan

It is essential to plan. Only with formal planning is it possible to share goals and organizational strategies. The Roman philosopher Seneca summarized it well when he said that "when sailing aimlessly, no wind is favorable."

In large companies, the existence of a corporate strategic plan is common, from which are defined tactical plans of the functional areas: finance, human resources, production, and marketing, among others. But in medium and small organizations, the marketing plan may appear as a single plan, as a guide for all the organization's strategic actions.

The marketing plan involves two groups of decisions: the strategic and the tactical. Strategic decisions concern the market in which the company intends to operate and the image or positioning it wants to adopt. Tactical decisions, on the other hand, refer to products, prices, distribution forms, and ways of company communication with the market.

Next, we propose a marketing plan template:

1. Identification of the goal

2. Defining the target market

3. Analysis of the environment

4. Definition of positioning strategy

5. Development, implementation, and control of the marketing mix product, price, distribution, and communication

6. Development of the action plan, with budgets

7. Definition of performance indicators for controlling the plan

Let's take each step separately:

1. *Identification of the goal:* This step is about the results expected to be achieved with the actions that will be implemented. The objectives can be expressed in sales, billing, profitability, and number of customers, among other forms.

2. *Defining the target market:* This step concerns the identification of the characteristics of effective customers to whom the company must sell. All decisions of product, price, distribution, and communication should be taken according to the profile of the target audience. The use of market research is useful and advisable at this time.

3. *Analysis of the environment:* Knowing the environment in which it operates gives the company the possibility to take actions that enable it to avoid threats and seize opportunities offered by the environment.

4. *Definition of positioning strategy:* By knowing the goals, the target market, and the environment, the company can set the institutional image with which it wants to establish itself in the market.

5. *Development, implementation, and control of the marketing mix:* This step concerns the tactical decisions regarding the marketing mix: product, price, distribution, and communication (promotion) of the company with its market. Depending on the size of the company, it is possible to develop a plan for each product or product line of the organization.

6. *Development of the action plan, with budgets:* This is the time to define each action, the person responsible for it, the budget, and the deadline by which the person responsible will have to develop the action.

7. *Definition of performance indicators for controlling the plan:* In this stage, numerical indicators are defined to measure the progress of actions and their real benefits to the company. The lack of such control measures and performance indicators generates difficulties commonly encountered during implementation of the plans: blown budgets, missed deadlines, and unreached goals, just to name a few.

Often, organizations opt for the presence of external consultants to develop and monitor the implementation of the marketing plan, which to succeed, requires the involvement of strategic groups of employees to lead the implementation of the actions, and the commitment of all for its effective execution.

Chapter 27
Market Positioning: You Must Choose One

Market positioning is the place that a product, company, or brand occupies in the minds of its customers. It is the development of a single offer, differentiated from the competition, whereby the brand will be identified in the market.

Source: www.shutterstock.com

Theories about positioning of organizations began among scholars of strategy, and have been popularized since 1980, with the launch of the book *Competitive Strategy* by Michael Porter.

In his book, Porter presented three generic strategies of positioning from which companies could choose:

- *Cost leadership:* The organization chooses to work at low prices in the conquest of its market;
- *Differentiation:* The organization strives to offer high quality, charging more for it; and
- *Focus:* With focus positioning, the company chooses to compete in a more specific segment of the market.

Porter argues that it is possible to combine focus with cost leadership, and focus with differentiation, but it is difficult, though possible, to combine differentiation with cost leadership.

In 1981, Al Ries and Jack Trout discussed the concept of positioning for marketing in their book *Positioning: The Battle for Your Mind.* The authors argued that the ultimate goal of positioning strategy is the building of strong brands through differentials that have meaning for its market.

The positioning process, today widespread among managers, may be determined in four steps:

1. The first step is *segmentation of the market,* that is, the selection of the target audience for which the company will drive its offer. It is important to know the target audience's profile, their values, and their interests.
2. Once the market is selected, the next step is *to define the value proposition,* the competitive differentiation that will motivate the customer choice and his loyalty to the brand. The competitive differential may be contained in the product itself, in services, in the presentation of the store,

in the experience provided to the customer, or in any other element that is unique and facilitates the identification and remembrance of the brand.

3. The third step is the *communication* of the positioning to the market through images and slogans that identify the brand personality.

4. The fourth step is *to stimulate the involvement of stakeholders* (employees, suppliers, customers, shareholders, managers, representatives, and distributors) in the construction and dissemination of the concept of the brand. As Urdan and Urdan (2010) stated, positioning is not just a matter of marketing, but affects the entire company. Everything the company does and how it does it should be aligned to its market positioning.

Today there is evidence that, even in a low competitive environment, brands that cannot develop their own identity, a personality, are not able to take their position and have more difficulty in succeeding. You have to share with the market the brand concept to achieve not only the mind, but also the heart, of the consumer.

Chapter 28
What Is the Ideal Business Model?

Every manager asks himself, "What is the ideal business model?" Market management has principles that are undeniably promoters of success, such as: diversified product mix, fair price, pleasant store environment, good communication with the market and with employees, and courteous service.

However, even with these basic principles, there is no single model of care, or shop, or price to please the customer. What exists is a single rule: There must be consistency between *the promise made to the market, the expectation that generates in the buyer*—in the market segment to which the promise was addressed and in which was generated buying and consumption interest—and *the effective delivery of the product or service*.

To better explain the countless possibilities of strategic postures that organizations can adopt in the market, we used the relation Price X Quality, expressed in the following matrix:

MATRIX
PRICE X QUALITY

PRICE

	HIGHER	**LOWER**
HIGHER	More for more	More for less
QUALITY		
LOWER	Less for more	Less for less

Source: Adapted from KOTLER & ARMSTRONG, 1995, p. 254.

The matrix shows four possible positioning strategies that organizations can adopt:

More for more: Choosing this positioning means having an offer of products and services of superior quality, whereby the company can charge prices above the market average. Customers, willing to pay, realize value on what they receive and become loyal to brands easily, in which case, they should be developed to become recommenders in the segment in which they operate.

More for less: This positioning is for those who manage to optimize their costs without compromising the quality of what they sell. They are ones that offer products and services of high quality with prices below the market average and have higher competitiveness; however, they run the risk of having a customer who buys only by price, vulnerable to any other better offer of the competition.

Source: www.shutterstock.com

Less for less: This positioning strategy is the opposite of the first one, but also honest. The company that chooses this position must clearly tell the market that they give up some additional comforts and services in order to reduce price. By the sincerity of the proposal, the customer raises his level of tolerance; he does not require anything above what was agreed upon, and even becomes loyal.

Less for more: This is a dangerous strategy of positioning. Offering inferior quality at a higher price only works when the customer does not know the options available in the market, and success only lasts until the customer realizes that he is being deceived.

As we can see, the ideal model does not exist. There will always be room for the luxury and the simple, for the selective and the popular, for the "tacky" and the "chic." The secret is in the appropriate choice of the target audience and in the coherence between what is promised and what is delivered to the market.

Chapter 29
Winning in the Market Despite the Crisis

From time to time, the world experiences the unpleasantness of an economic crisis, now globalized. We must recognize, however, that regardless of the difficulties that arise in the market, companies should continue existing, producing and selling.

Source: www.shutterstock.com

The question that arises is: How threatened, in fact, is your company when facing a crisis?

To answer this question, we must first understand that threat is not simply an unfavorable situation in the market. Threat is the result of the meeting of unfavorable situations of the environment with weak points of the organization:

THREAT = UNFAVORABLE SITUATION + WEAKNESSES

We also have to think about opportunities, which are not only favorable in the market. Opportunities are configured through the encounter of favorable situations with the strong points of the companies:

OPPORTUNITY= FAVORABLE SITUATION + STRENGHTS

Thus, a company that always cautiously managed its financial resources through cost control and margin of contribution of its products; invested in staff training, encouraging the talent of its employees; was attentive to the quality of its offerings in the market, to conform to the expectations generated in its buyers and consumers; and constantly developed marketing actions to win clients and their loyalty certainly will not be as threatened by unfavorable situations of the environment as those organizations that accumulated weaknesses.

On the other hand, for companies that are actually endangered, the crisis can also be a good moment to identify those weak points and develop new management practices, especially for marketing.

It is in a crisis situation that companies realize how little they know their customers.

At this time it is possible, for example, to invest in the construction of a database of customers, perhaps using already existing information at the company but which was never used for relationship marketing. The proximity with customers, individuals or companies, generates loyalty and warrants business continuity in times of crisis.

The company that controls its costs, invests in its employees, and plans its marketing actions, continually researching the behavior of its customers, knowing their needs and desires, offering them the right product, and adding services that create value perception, will rarely be threatened by crisis. It can, yes, be experiencing unfavorable situations that require caution, but its strong points will keep it firmly in the market.

Chapter 30
Finally, Some Advice

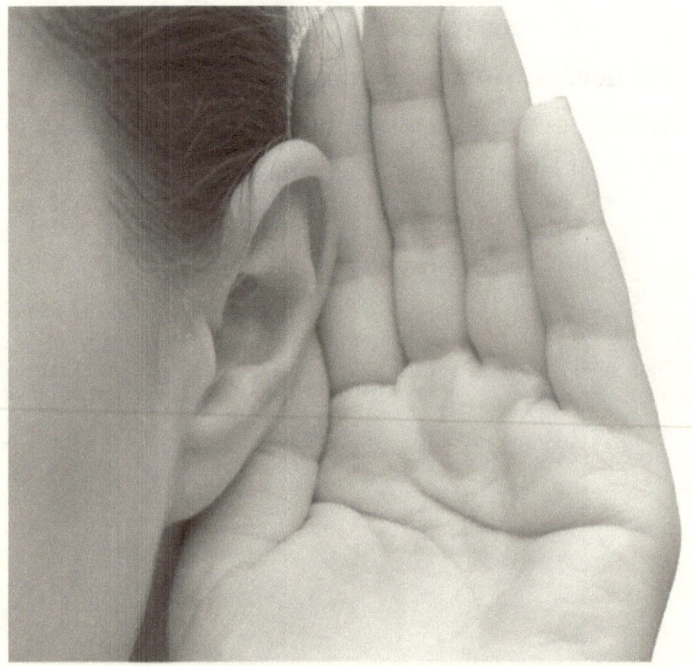

Source: www.shutterstock.com

Creativity is the keyword. Be creative in attracting and retaining your customers. Here are some final suggestions:

1. Try to observe the behavior of your customers. Knowing their needs and desires, it becomes easier to serve them and enchant them.
2. Create a wellness environment in your company through temperature, scents, colors, and music.

3. Respect and fairly remunerate your employees. They are the points of contact between your company and your customers.

4. Along the same lines, empower your employees for good attendance, which means in addition to technique, spontaneity, creativity, and good humor.

5. Create additional services that add value to what you sell. Enchant the customer and encourage him to come back, bringing other customers.

6. Enhance the presentation of your products; the purchase begins by looking.

Finally, avoid getting discouraged in your business. Words have power as well as thoughts and actions. And always study! Experience is important, but the market is constantly changing, challenging us to learn the new in order to evolve continuously.

Bibliography and Suggested Reading

AMA (American Marketing Association). *The American Marketing Association Releases New Definition for Marketing*, Chicago, IL, Jan. 14, 2008.

Bach, David; Allen, David B. Cuidado com o Nonmarket. *HSM Management*, No. 82, pp. 112-118, Sept. / Oct. 2010.

Borden, Neil. "The Concept of the Marketing Mix." In: *Journal of Advertising Research. Classics*, vol. II, Sept. 1984.

Celestino, Nadja M. Nara *et al. Os Fenômenos Balking e Reneging como Motivo de Desistência de Compra*. Article presented at 6º Latin American Congress of Retail—CLAV, FGV / São Paulo 2012.

Engel, J. F.; Blackwell, R. D.; Miniard, P. W. *Comportamento do Consumidor.* 8. ed. Rio de Janeiro: LTC, 2008.

Ferrel, O. C.; Hartline, Michael D. *Estratégia de Marketing.* São Paulo: Cengage Learning, 2009.

Furtado, Beth. *Desejos Contemporâneos (Contemporary Wishes).* São Paulo: Gouvêa de Souza & MD, 2008.

Grönroos, Christian. "Quo Vadis Marketing? Toward a Relationship Marketing Paradigm." *Journal of Marketing Management*, 1994, 10, pp. 347-360.

Haight, F. A. "Queuing with balking." *Biometrika—Oxford Journals*, vol. 44, no. 3/4, 1957, pp. 360-369.

Karsaclian, E. *Comportamento do Consumidor.* 2. ed. São Paulo: Atlas, 2004.

Kotler, Philip. "Atmospherics as a Marketing Tool." *Journal of Retailing*, Greenwich, v. 49, no. 4, pp. 48-64, 1973.

Kotler, Philip; Armstrong, Gary. *Princípios de Marketing*. Rio de Janeiro: Brazil's Prentice Hall, 1995.

Kotler, Philip; Keller, Kevin L. *Marketing Management*. 12. ed. New Jersey: Pearson-Prentice Hall, 2006.

Levitt, Theodore. *A imaginação de marketing*. São Paulo: Atlas, 1985.

Lovelock, Christopher; Wirtz, Jochen. *Marketing de serviços: pessoas, tecnologias e resultados*. São Paulo: Pearson Prentice Hall, 2006.

Mason, Barry; Mayer, Morris L.; Wilkinson, J. B. *Modern Retailing: Theory and Practice*. 6. ed. Homewood, IL: Richard D. Irwin, 1993.

McCarthy, E. Jerome; Perreault, William D. Jr. *Basic Marketing: A Managerial Approach*. Homewood, IL: Richard D. Irwin, 1960.

McDonald, Malcolm. *Planos de Marketing: como criar e implementar planos eficazes*. Rio de Janeiro: Elsevier, 2004.

Parente, Juracy. *Varejo no Brasil*. São Paulo: Atlas, 2000.

Popcorn, Faith. *The Popcorn Report*. New York: HarperCollins, 1992.

Porter, Michael. *Estratégia competitiva (Competitive Strategy)*. Rio de Janeiro: Campus, 1980.

Porter, Michael; Kramer, Mark R. "Criação de valor compartilhado." *Harvard Business Review*, Jan. 2011, pp. 17-32.

Ries, Al; Trout, Jack. *Posicionamento: a batalha pela sua mente (Positioning: The Battle for Your Mind)*. Porto Alegre: Makron Books, 1981.

Solomon, M. R. *O comportamento do consumidor: comprando, possuindo e sendo*. 5. ed. Porto Alegre: Bookman, 2002.

Torres, Ana Carolina C.; Buhamra, Cláudia. "O aroma como componente de geração de valor de marca e de varejo." *REBRAE—Revista Brasileira de Estratégia*, Curitiba, Vol. 4, no. 3, pp. 211-222, Sept. / Dec. 2011.

United Nations Report. *The World's Women 2010: Trends and Statistics*. United Nations Publication, New York, 2010.

Urdan, Andrew T.; Urdan, Flávio T. *Marketing estratégico no Brasil*. São Paulo: Atlas, 2010.

Weyne, Alfredo B.; Buhamra, Cláudia. "Os efeitos do móbile marketing como instrumento de promoção de vendas." Article presented at 2º Latin American Congress of Retail—CLAV, FGV / São Paulo 2009.

Researched Websites

The Economist. http://www.economist.com/node/15174418. "Female Power," Dec 30, 2009.

HSM Management. www.hsm.com.br/editorias/mobile-marketing-deve-movimentar-us-24-bi.

IBGE (Instituto Brasileiro de Geografia e Estatística). "Censo 2010." www.censo2010.ibge.gov.br.

www.shutterstock.com. Authorized photos.

Malozzi, Maria Fernanda. *Consumidor mostra Resistência à Publicidade Mobile*. Propmark, BloGift, Fey, 2010. http://www3.propmark.com.br

Cláudia Buhamra is undergraduate in Business Administration from Federal University of Ceará (FEAAC/UFC); master and doctorate in Business Administration with concentration on Marketing from FGV-EAESP (Getúlio Vargas Foundation—School of Business Administration of São Paulo). She completed the master's degree at the London Business School in England and did the post doctorate at the John Molson School of Business of Concordia University, in Montreal, Canada. She is a professor of Marketing, on the Faculty of Economics, Management, Actuarial and Accounting, at Federal University of Ceará (FEAAC/UFC), where she held the positions of coordinator of Professional Master's Degree in Business Administration, coordinator of the Specialization Course Manager of Marketing, and head of the Department of Administration. She is speaker and author of works presented and published in Brazil and abroad. She is a partner at the consulting firm of Buhamra & Romero Strategic Solutions.

Retail Marketing Management: Concepts, Guidelines, and Practices

Born from studies and the experiences of its author, *Retail Marketing Management* provides guidelines, concepts, and practices of marketing, with a special focus on retail management. The guidelines aim to encourage and facilitate the development of marketing strategies that enable organizations to achieve greater competitive power and build brands that are respected and valued in the market, while the concepts are intended to give the theoretical background to the practices commented on and suggested here.

As the language is accessible and direct, the work has the advantage of proposing immediate solutions for business, especially for market professionals who are eager for results and have no time for heavy academic reading.

Moreover, the teachings contained herein are also useful to students and teachers who wish to enhance their knowledge about marketing.

Application

This book is recommended for professionals and academics from different areas and can be used for reading in business environments, and as part of the literature of technology courses for undergraduate and postgraduate studies in business administration and marketing.